Supernatural Experiences

Supernatural Experiences

Paul Blankenburg

Paul A. Blankenburg

CONTENTS

Books by Paul A. Blankenburg

INTRODUCTION

There has been a debate going on for centuries about Supernatural powers. They show themselves in different ways, to different people, under different circumstances. Some people say they are evil and other people say they are for good. You will have to decide for yourself how you will judge them in these two stories.

Do you believe in the power of the Supernatural? If you do, then after reading these two stories your belief will be re-enforced. If you doubt that the Supernatural exists, then after you read these two stories you might decide to change your mind.

These two stories were told to me by my father and mother, and I am sure that as witnesses to the first story and as a major part of the second story, they told me the truth. That is not like hearing it second or third hand, but it is from the horse's mouth, so to speak.

All the names of the people in both of these stories are the real names of the people involved. All the names of the places, towns, businesses and ranches in these two stories are the real names that they are called.

These two stories are true, and I have written as accurately an account of them as I can and as they were told to me.

Paul A. Blankenburg
January 17, 2023
Van Horn, Texas

332-2637 A LOVE STORY BITTER-SWEET
Their Journey

SUPERNATURAL EXPERIENCES
ISBN # 979-8-218-14106-6

A True Story About a Supernatural Happening

This book is dedicated to my Grandchildren so they will know some of the stories told by their Great Grandparents.

TABLE OF CONTENTS
IT HAPPENED IN: "ELCAMPO, TEXAS" #1

IT HAPPENED IN: "ELCAMPO, TEXAS" #2

"IT HAPPENED: In El Campo, Texas" #1

CHAPTER ONE-THE BEGINNING

The background for this true story begins many years before the actual story starts in 1938. Therefore, I will have to go back to the era before World War 1, to lay the framework for this story, so you will be able to understand how the characters and events of the story actually line up to bring them to an astounding conclusion that might give you chills and something to think about at the end.

L.A. McWilliams, my grandfather on my mother's side, sold out his homestead in the Cherokee Strip in Woods County, Oklahoma in May of 1908 and moved in June 1908 to 320 acers of land he bought, to farm rice and ranch cattle, eighteen miles southeast of El Campo, Wharton County, Texas, in the five corners area known locally as the Blue Creek area. My mother Velma was only two months old at the time and she and her older sister Florence grew up there on that farm in a small house that my grandfather built himself. Five families including the McWilliams family moved at the same time from Oklahoma and bought land close together there in the Blue Creek area. They were basically in an unsettled wilderness that was waist high in prairie grass with no improvements and no neighbors. There were some large ranches close to them and cowboys from those ranches would stop by their farm to visit from time to time and maybe share some news of the area.

There was the East KO Ranch a few miles to the west

of them, the Northern Headquarters Ranch to the south of them and the Blue Creek Ranch to the east of them that went all the way to the west side of the Colorado River and the A.H. "Shanghai" Pierce Ranch to the north of them. These ranches each covered thousands and thousands of acers and each had many Cowboys that were made up of Mexican Vaquero's that had been the offspring of the Mexican Rancheros from the days of the Spanish Missions at Goliad, Texas, Blacks that had been offspring from Slaves that had worked the Plantations on the east side of the Colorado River and Caney Creek and found out that they excelled as Cowboys after being taught the skill by the Mexicans and the offspring of European Emigrants that were also taught the skill by the Mexicans. These Cowboys taught my Grandfather McWilliams a lot about the Texas way to raise cattle. They would hire out to him on a pay-by-the-day basis to help build fences, work cows and help with odd jobs. They also gave him much needed knowledge of how to make home remedies to treat cattle diseases and how to be able to diagnose what kind of sickness the animal had. They taught my grandfather how to smoke cure meat and make sausage that he had never known before, because his relatives had not known how to do it. They would camp close to the McWilliams house sometimes overnight and my grandfather would join them at their campfire and listen to the stories of the old days that the Mexican Cowboys would talk about, when the Spanish owned the land and of the Texian revolt from Mexico and their fight for independence. The Black Cowboys would tell stories about their relatives who worked on the plantations around the town of Wharton, Texas on the east side of the Colorado river and at Egypt, Texas and at Iago, Texas along Caney Creek with the rich red soil deposited by the centuries of flooding of the Colorado river. The White Cowboys would tell their stories of what European Countries their parents and grandparents had emigrated from, why they had left there and how they found their way to Texas. One of the Cowboys that came by the most often was a 6-foot 2 inch, longed legged, lanky, sandy-red headed young man that had been born in Danevang, Texas a Danish settlement that was settled in the late 1800's by Danish immigrants. His parents were farmers, but he never liked farming, and he started working part time for the Ranches until he honed his Cowboy skills and became a full time Cowboy for the Blue Creek Ranch. His name was Ben Peterson. Ben seemed to always be in good humor and was ready to help anyone if they needed it. He made friends easily and quickly with the Cowboys he worked with and the new settlers that came to the area. He was always very interested in the stories around the campfires and the stories he heard from the new people that came to settle in the area, because he considered these stories as another form of education that broadened his knowledge of the world. Ben was particularly interested and attentive when the Mexican Cowboys were telling stories of when Spain owned Texas and of the Mexican Revolution from Spain and then the colonization of then Tejas by the Gringos, white Nortino's, from the U.S. and finally the rule of General Santa Ana and the Revolution that the Texians won that gave them their independence from Mexico. These Mexican Cowboys knew all the stories about the battles from the Mexican side, so that gave Ben much more information than he had received from his school days. When the Mexican Cowboys told the story about the Mexican Army following Sam Houston and the Texian Army to San Jacinto, they told the story that General Antonio Lopez De Santa Anna, before he had the Mexican Army ford the Colorado River to the east side, south of the town of Wharton, he ordered that two cannon be filled with Mexican gold and silver coins and plugged the muzzles, then buried on the west side of the river bank between two huge oak trees. He had a blaze chopped on each tree to mark the location of the burial site. This was the payroll for the Mexican Army that he was to give them after they won the battle and defeated the rebellious Texicans. They lost the battle, and the cannon were never retrieved, so this treasure still lay buried on the west side of the Colorado River that was now part of the Blue Creek Ranch that Ben Peterson was working for, and it started his lifelong search for this Mexican treasure.

Ever-time Ben got a chance he would ride his horse on a different section of the west bank of the Colorado River trying to find the two big oak trees with the blaze chopped on each to identify the location of the buried Mexican treasure. In places there would be so much thick brush and mustang grape vines that he would have to get off his horse tie him to a tree and walk in order to investigate a certain spot that was too thick to ride into and he would have to walk slow, to also look for poisonous snakes that would live in that thick brushy area. He would smell the musky odor of the big timber rattlesnakes and the big cotton mouth moccasins before he could see them, so he had time to draw his Colt pistol and shoot them as he discovered their hiding place. These big snakes always made him shudder a little bit, because he had seen cowboys that had been bitten by them and how bad they had suffered and sometimes died from their poison. He found traces, now and then, that the Mexican Army had left behind, such as a lost Mexican spur, a button from a Mexican Army uniform and one time even a knife with a Mexican silver handle topped with a silver eagle, but he never located the mythical oak trees with their blazes. Ben had cleaned these artifacts up, so he could admire them better and he would carefully rub his hands over them trying to get a feeling for what kind of man each had belonged to. He was especially fond of the big knife and after he cleaned it up, he discovered that there were some initials engraved on the handle in Spanish design that was very elaborate with a lot of flourishes and also the blade when honed sharp held its edge very good, so he made a sheath for it, and he wore the knife on his belt, and it became a part of his everyday personal equipment. It was noticed by many people that asked him about his very unusual knife and he would relate the story of how he had found it. He tried to figure out what the initials stood for but was never sure about their meaning. He had questioned several Mexican Cowboys through the years as to the truth of the story about the buried cannons full of Mexican gold and silver coins and everyone swore that the story was the truth, because it had come down to them by their family, and that they surely wouldn't have told them a lie. This just reenforced Ben to be even more resolute in his search. He even made himself a sort of a map of the location of each artifact that he found from the Mexican

Army so he might to be able to find the trail that they made, and he could follow it to the two huge oak trees with the blazes chopped on them, but he always lost the trail, because it never went far enough to the Colorado Riverbank. The years went by, and he was starting to get some gray in his hair and some wrinkles in his face and neck from all of the harsh weather that he worked in as a Cowboy, but unable to admit defeat Ben still kept up his search unwilling to give up on his dream of finding the Mexican treasure. Now it has become more of a test of will than a lust for riches. He just knew that someday, maybe even tomorrow he would discover the long-lost hiding place of that fabulous Mexican treasure.

During these years Ben kept his friendship with my Grand-father Mr. McWilliams and his family and he visited them even after they moved into the town of El Campo, when he came to town for supplies or for some local celebration that the town was having, because life on the ranch was devoid of any entertainment other than the Cowboys pulling pranks on each other whenever they could, so as to liven up the ranch life a bit. Ben had worked on the Blue Creek Ranch since he had been just a youth and he had become a very accomplished and trustworthy Cowboy, so he was finally promoted to be, the Ranch Forman which was a very responsible position that required a lot of dedication and good judgement in keeping the ranch running smoothly with the ranch work and also with dealing with the Cowboys, which was sometimes a real trial, because of their natural trait of being independent and naturally wild when it came to enjoying themselves. Many times, he would have to solve disagreements between them and sometimes in a rather rough way to get their attention. Many of the Cowboys were drifters, so no one ever really knew if they were using their real names and they never let much to be known about their lives, not even where they had been born. The main thing Been needed to know about them was if they could ride well, rope well and if they were strong enough and tough enough to work long hours in a lot of harsh weather and if they could take orders from him. If some of this was missing from their character, then they wouldn't last very long working on the Blue Creek Ranch. Once in a while a really young boy would wander up looking for a job. Usually, his clothes would be ragged, and his shoes worn out and he would be hungry and dirty from living rough in the open. Ben would talk to him and try to figure out why he was wandering around out on the open range by himself, a lot of times with only a strong stick and a knife. Most of the time Ben got the story that the boy ran away when his family was traveling in a wagon and he finally got tired of being beaten by a mean, drunken stepfather and he stole away at night while the rest of them were sleeping. Usually if Ben was satisfied with the boy's story, he would put him to work at the Ranch Head Quarters doing odd jobs, that gave Ben time to ask around El Campo if anyone knew anything about the boy, because Ben usually didn't go into town but once a month. If the boy was a good worker and he took orders good, then after a few months Ben would ask around town if anyone needed a young boy to help them and usually, he could find the boy a place that would furnish him with room and board and a small wage. A couple of these young boys worked out real-good in El Campo and became good citizens and Ben would go and visit them when he came to town for supplies and to visit the McWilliams family.

As the range around the big ranches began to be settled by Homesteaders that had to fence their property, because the Texas law didn't make the ranchers fence in their grazing range. In order for the Homesteaders to keep the cattle from destroying their crops they had to fence in their property with barbed wire. This started to preset a problem for the big ranches, because often the Homesteaders had property that were adjacent to each other for miles and the fences were connected and the big ranches had to start buying a lot of land that they used to graze just to keep a large grazing range in one piece. Homesteaders and then other Settlers came in that had sold out their land in other States to take advantage of the cheap land in Wharton County, Texas. This is what my Grandfather McWilliams and four other families did in 1908 after selling their homesteads in Oklahoma. All of this brought prosperity to the town of El Campo, because of the increase in agriculture crops other than cattle and hay. These new farmers were farming cotton, corn, rice and some were even planting orchards of pecans, peaches, plums and pears. All of this was being harvested and brought into El Campo to be sold to buyers from other places and it generated hundreds of jobs and created the building of many businesses that processed and stored these products. These farms also changed the way that the ranches had to operate, and they had to increasingly have their pastures in separate places that were fenced, if they were going to graze a large number of cattle. This made the ranches have to work each pasture separately and sell the cattle from each pasture separately instead of having one big roundup twice a year. The big ranches slowly started to get smaller, and the farming area got larger and many of the Cowboys that had worked on the big ranches started out on their own with small herds on a small, leased pasture and a job on the side in El Campo. This shift in the way the land was divided up gave rise to many new people being involved in both farming and ranching on a small basis. Then oil was discovered and many of the small landowners became very wealthy and they started other businesses using the money that they were paid as royalty for the oil production on their land. All of these changes brought a lot of wealth to El Campo until the Depression that started with the Stock Market crash and that put a lot of the smaller farmers and ranchers out of business, if they had browed money on their land, because the price they got for their crops and cattle was so small that it would not support loan and interest payments. All of this eventually affected Blue Creek Ranch and with it, Ben Peterson. The ranch started to sell off some of its large herd of cattle after losing a lot of the open range grazing land and they then had to dismiss some of their Cowboys, because they were no longer needed with the reduced herd. Ben still worked for the ranch, but he could see the writing on the wall that the time of the big ranches on the coastal plain in Wharton County was about over. He had saved his money wisely and he had enough to buy a small place of his own and a small house there. This land was located just a couple of miles Northeast of El Campo. It was a good spot that allowed him to be able to improve it on his time off from the Blue Creek Ranch. It's close proximately to El Campo also gave him more time to be able to visit his friends that lived in town and that included my Grandfather Mr. McWilliams and also his daughter Velma that had now married C.T. (Blackie) Blankenburg. Velma and Blackie, my future Mother and Father, were living with Mr. McWilliams in the old house that he bought after he had sold out his farm and moved to town and started his little Mac's Fix-it Shop. When Ben would be working and staying out at the Blue Creek Ranch, he usually still found time to search for the elusive Mexican treasure cannons. He had never lost his desire to find them although from time to time he would be discouraged and tell himself that they just didn't exist, no matter that the Mexican Cowboys had sworn that they did. He really just couldn't face the notion that it had all been something that he had built up in his mind that finding the cannons was not a reality. He had been searching for them for so many years that it had become a part of his mental routine like a habit that you perform without thinking about. It just happens when time presents itself and is automatically performed without even thing about what you are going to do. This is how Ben kept looking for that Mexican treasure of gold and silver. Looking for them had been a part of him since he had been just a youth sitting around the campfire listening to the stories being told by the Mexican Cowboys and it was ingrained into his mind just as much as the arithmetic, he had learned in school 2+2=4. He had never done anything crazy like ignoring his responsibilities at work on the Blue Creek Ranch to look for the two Mexican cannon's. He just used his time off to do that and he even had friends that would give him ideas about their location from things that they had read on the subject, because everyone that knew him were aware that he had been looking for the Mexican Treasure for many years. This was no secret and everyone that knew Ben was aware of it. Talking about the two cannons filled with Mexican gold and silver coins was always a topic of the conversation when they were talking to Ben. When in El Campo Ben, from time to time, would visit the local Library and check out every book he could find and read about the Texas Revolution with Mexico to see if he could glean any further information on that subject that would give him more clues as to the treasure's location. Nothing he learned seemed to fill in the blanks that he needed to put the whole picture together to find their location. Ben still felt that someday somehow, he would come across the information that he needed and maybe it would even reveal itself in a way that he would never expect. This is how Ben kept holding out hope that something somehow would give him a hot trail that he could follow.

CHAPTER TWO-El Campo

My Grandfather held on to his farm after the Stock Market crash of 1929 and the Depression years until 1933 when he no longer could justify farming at a loss, so he sold out for what he could get for the farm and the livestock and farm implements, paid his debts and used what money he had left to buy an old house on a 60-foot x 100-foot lot in El Campo, Texas. My Grandfathers wife Beulah, my grandmother, had died in 1926 and my mother's older sister Florance had married and was teaching school at Tomball, Texas. My Mother Velma had been living in El Campo, Texas for several years, with town friends, finishing her High School, getting her teaching certificate and working as a Teacher and a Coach. He also rented a small run-down building on Monserrate Street to start a business he named Mc's Fixit Shop, because he was good with his hands and was known to be honest and did good work, he soon had a small business that provided him with a subsistence living. My mother moved there with him and was teaching school at Plainview, a country school just a few miles southwest of El Campo where she drove to everyday in the 1929 Model A Ford Coupe that she had proudly bought new with her teacher's salary of $60.00 a month.

El Campo was a growing town on the Gulf Coast prairie just 36 miles inland from Palacios Bay in 1933, in spite of the hard times produced by the Depression. The location of the town of El Campo was on the old path that the Spanish Traders took from Mexico through then called Tejas (Texas) on their way to Louisiana to trade. There were many of these routes through Texas used for trade and for the Spanish Government at Mexico City to resupply it's Mission system and Presidio Military Garrisons. These routes or roads were officially called Comino Reals (Royal Roads) and this one came across the Rio Grande, called the Rio Bravo at that time, at Matamoros, Mexico and wandered through south Texas to their Mission Espiritu de Santo and their Presidio and Mission LA Bahia located at Goliad, Texas then on to the old town of Victoria, Texas on the Guadalupe River from there to the future location of El Campo and on to a ford crossing of the Colorado River, south of the future location of the town of Wharton, Texas, on the way east to Louisiana.

The future location of El Campo on this vast Coastal Plane, that was almost treeless except around the creeks and rivers that traversed it on their way to the Gulf of Mexico would have been impossible to locate until the building of the railroad. The town of El Campo sprang up at a location called Prairie Switch, because there was a switch there that gave the train access to a sidetrack that went to a set of cattle pens that were used to load cattle on to the train to be shipped for market and also a loading dock to load prairie hay into box cars to be shipped east. The Mexican Cowboys renamed this location El Campo, meaning "The Camp", simply because they would camp here for days with the herds of cattle loading them on the train and the name stuck for a permanent name of the town. El Campo grew out of this to become a respectable town that was known to be interested in advancement with new business that were owned by new people in town and not like some other towns that suppressed the ownership of businesses by new people that would create competition against the old wealthy families of the town. El Campo was moving toward the idea of progress.

CHAPTER THREE-THE CHANCE MEETING

Ben saw this evolution of El Campo, because he had seen El Campo in its early days when it was just a railroad track spur that allowed for a big set of cattle pens and a loading dock to load and ship cattle and hay with very few small houses and small businesses that were needed at that time. Now it was a bustling and growing town with almost everything you needed to live a nice life. This is why he decided to buy his place just on the outskirts of El Campo, because he was no longer a high-spirited youth. Ben was aware that he was witnessing the end of the era of big ranching and with that it would eventually be the end of his job on the Blue Creek Ranch and in El Campo, he had friends that he wanted to be close to and that as he got older, he would be able to live there more easily. This was the more practicable side to Ben Peterson.

As time went on there was less and less work to do at the Blue Creek Ranch, but Ben was still on their payroll to take care of the things that were needed to keep the much smaller ranch running as smoothly as possible. This allowed Ben to spend more time at the place that he bought getting it fixed up for his permanent residence and also for the small herd of cattle that he maintained there. That gave Ben more time to visit his friends in town and with this he visited Mr. McWilliams and his daughter Velma and her husband Blackie Blankenburg. Blackie owned a small gasoline filling station on the main street in El Campo where he sold gasoline and oil, fixed tires and bought used tires that still had enough rubber on them so he could cut new treads on them and resell them. There was a good market for this with the depression limiting everyone's income. He was clearing $40.00 per month and Velma, his wife, was making $60.00 per month teaching school at a country school southeast of El Campo known as Plainview School. Together they had been investing in some bull calves that a local Dairy were selling for $1.00 each and putting four at a time on a nurse cow and then when they got big enough, they would sell them and buy some more, and this grew to where Blackie had leased a small pasture just south of El Campo and was now running a few cows himself along with the filling station. When Ben would come to their house to visit many times, he would be invited to share a meal with them and he was very delighted to do so, because Velma was a very accomplished cook, and he enjoyed the meal and conversation with his longtime friends.

Mr. McWilliams, Velma and Blackie had next door neighbors they made good friends with by the name of Harper. The Harper's were about the same age as Velma and Blackie, and he worked in the oil field for Texaco that was drilling a lot of oil wells on the Pierce Ranch. On Mr. Harpers days off they would visit, and Blackie would catch up on what was happening in the oil business. Mrs. Harper had lost her diamond wedding ring a couple months before and Blackie and Velma had tried to help them find it. They looked everywhere they thought it might be found and had almost torn the house apart looking for it. Mr. Harper told his wife not to worry that he would get her another one someday, but she was not interested in another ring. She told him that it wouldn't be the same thing, because the one she lost had been the ring that he had placed on her finger at their wedding, and he had surprised her with it when they had very little money and she didn't think that he could afford a ring with a diamond in it. No other ring was going to do for her, and she was very upset that they had not found it. When the Harpers came over to visit that was usually the topic of conversation and trying to think of other places to look for the ring.

One Saturday at lunch time Ben Peterson came to visit Mr. McWilliams, Velma and Blackie. After lunch Velma gave Ben a small book, she came across that had been translated into English from Spanish. This translation had been originally a journal written in Spanish that had belonged to a Mexican Capitan that had fought at the battle of San Jacinto, and he had kept a record of his time in Texas during the war. They were discussing this book when the Harper's knocked on their door and came in for a visit. They had with them a friend of theirs that was a little intoxicated. He was a salesman for a tool company and had traveled around to many towns doing his job. He had discovered that an old Black woman who lived in Victoria, Texas about fifty-five miles southwest of El Campo, was recommended to him by an acquaintance, and she was reported to be a recognized Fortune Teller that had produced some results for people he knew. They had come over ask Blackie if he wanted to ride with them to Victoria to talk to the Fortune Teller and see if she could tell them where the diamond wedding ring was. Their intoxicated friend was a little sarcastic about going to consult with a Fortune Teller, because he didn't believe in Fortune Tellers. He thought of them all as being nothing more than lying charlatans that took advantage of people that had run out of options for solving a problem and taking their money in the process. Mr. Harper was determined to go and talk to the Fortune Teller anyway to see what she could tell him about the possible whereabouts of his wife's wedding ring. Blackie told them that he didn't think that he wanted to ride all the way to Victoria. All the time that the Harpers were talking about the Fortune Teller, Ben Peterson had been thinking and he thought why he never came up with something like that. It was such a simple thing to think of and it had never entered his mind. He had heard about Fortune Tellers for years and some people believed in then and other people didn't, it was as simple as that. Ben asked Mr. Harper if he could ride along, because he wanted to ask that Fortune Teller about the Mexican cannons that he had been looking for since his youth. Mr. Harper was glad for him to accompany them to Victoria, so Ben, Mr. Harper and his intoxicated friend got in Mr. Harpers' 1935 Ford Sedan and drove to Victoria. Mr. Harpers intoxicated friend had his fun with them kidding them about how stupid they were for making this trip for nothing and giving their money away to this old Black woman when they could go to a good beer hall and have a good time drinking a few cold beers. Ben and Mr. Harper just ignored him and kept their thoughts to them-selves. When they got to Victoria the intoxicated friend was giving Mr. Harper instructions on how to find the house of the old Black woman, that he had obtained from a man that had visited her there. They wound around on some old streets south of the railroad tracks and finally found her house. It had taken a lot of time to drive to Victoria and to find her house, so it was now getting into the dusk of evening. Her house was a very old one-story house built the old fashion way with 1x12 planks lined up vertically and the seams between them were sealed over with 1x4 boards to keep out the rain and wind. Most of the paint on the house had weathered away long ago and the porch was leaning to one side a bit. The front yard was mostly dirt like a school yard where children had played and worn the grass off. The front door was open, and a light was showing inside through the screen door. Mr. Harper turned off the motor and the three of them walked up the uneven sidewalk made of old bricks. They stepped on the porch and the floor planks gave some creaks and Mr. Harper knocked on the screen door. An old Black woman came to the door and turned on the porch light. Mr. Harper asked her if she was the Fortune Teller, and she was quiet for a while not saying a word just looking them over really good then she pointed her finger at the intoxicated man and told him that he could not come in because he had been making fun of her all of the way over on their trip and that he should go back and sit in the car. This astonished them, because how on earth could she have known this. The intoxicated man went back to the car and then she asked Mr. Harper and Ben if they each had $5.00, because that is what she charged for her services. They both showed her their money and then she opened the screen door and let them into the front room. She took their money and asked them which of them was to be the first for her to talk to and Mr. Harper told her that he was to go first, and she led him through a door that had been closed into a small room and she closed the door behind him. Ben sat in a wooden chair in the front room waiting his turn. It was a sparsely furnished room with very old wooden furniture and the walls and ceiling were covered in wallpaper that had some stains from leaking water, but the room was clean and smelled only of old wood and furnishings. Mr. Harper was in the room with the old Black woman for about thirty minutes when he came out and he had a smile on his face that gave Ben some confidence that he was about to find out exactly where the Mexican cannons that contained all of those Mexican gold and silver coins were to be found. He even had a pencil and paper to write down the directions that she was to give him, so he would not have a chance to forget any of it. She motioned for Ben to come into the small room, and he got up and followed her. She closed the door behind him and motioned him to a wood chair across the smell wood table from her. He introduced himself to her and she was quiet for a time, just looking into his eyes. Ben noticed that she had gray eyes which were very unusual for a Black woman to have, because almost all of the Black people either had black or brown eyes. Those gray eyes of hers seemed to stare right into his brain and it gave him a kind of dizzy feeling. Then she just nodded her head toward him slowly, so he began to tell her that he was there to get the location of the Mexican cannon's that had been buried on the west bank of the Colorado River during the Texas war of Independence from Mexico. The old Back woman just kept looking into his eyes with those gray eyes of hers, not even blinking. When he was through talking, she just chuckled a little and the next thing she said Ben had a hard time grasping it at first, because it was something that was so far from his mind in what he had thought that she would say that he was dumbfounded or a minute. The old Black Fortune Teller was smiling, and she told Ben that she had already known why he had come to see her. She told Ben that the Mexican cannon's, were there alright buried on that west bank of the Colorado River just like the Mexican Cowboys had told him the story of them so many years ago. She told Ben that he could have saved himself a lot of work and time if he had come to her years ago to find out about them. Then the next thing that she told Ben almost knocked him out of his chair. She looked at Ben again with those gray eyes and told him that she knew exactly the location of those Mexican cannon's, with that fabulous treasure inside of them, but that she was not going to tell him where to find them, because they did not belong to him. She told him that if the true owner of them came to her she would tell him how to find them. She said that the true owner of the Mexican treasure would be someone that was a direct descendent of a Mexican Soldier that had fought in the war and that she would know who he was when he came to her. The next thing that the Fortune Teller told Ben astounded Ben Peterson and it put chills all over his body. She told him that he had come close to finding the fabulous Mexican treasure, because he had ridden his horse over it several times. The Black woman then got up from her chair, which signaled that the visit was over. Ben got up with a rather disgruntled look on his face and they filed out of the room into the front room where he and Mr.

Harper then went out the front screen door to the car. Ben looked back at the house when he got onto Mr. Harper's car and the Black woman was standing inside the screen door looking at him with those gray eyes. Ben wondered what she was thinking.

The intoxicated friend of Mr. Harper woke up when they got into the car. He asked if they thought that they had spent their money wisely and Mr. Harper told him that they would see when they got back to El Campo and Ben just stayed quiet. On the drive back to El Campo Ben had a lot of time to think about what the Fortune Teller had told him, because the intoxicated man had fallen back to sleep in the moving car, and it was quiet. Mr. Harper didn't have much to say either and Ben supposed that he was thinking about his experience with the Black woman also.

CHAPTER FOUR-SEARCH FOR THE DIAMOND RING

They pulled into the driveway of Mr. Harper's house and his wife was over at Mr. McWilliams house and she along with Mr. McWilliams, Velma and Blackie came out to meet them and to hear the story about what had transpired on their trip and if they had found the Black woman Fortune Teller. Mr. Harper told them that they had found her alright. Then he proceeded to tell them about his experience with her, but Ben was quiet. They asked Ben about his experience and all he said was that he would tell them later. Mr. Harper told his wife to go into their house and get the flashlight, because they were going to need it to look for her diamond wedding ring. They all went over to the Harpers' house and Mr. Harper told them that supposedly the ring had fallen off of his wife's finger as she was walking down the front sidewalk and it had lodged itself in a crack in the sidewalk and there, he would find it. His wife brought the flashlight out to him, and they all walked slowly down the sidewalk looking down at the beam of light searching for the crack in the sidewalk. Suddenly the crack appeared out of the darkness and Mr. Harper moved the flashlight back and forth slowly until the beam rested on something that sparkled in the light. He reached in his pocket and pulled out his pocketknife and opened the small blade in it. He asked Blackie if he would hold the light while he knelt down to see if he could retrieve the object from the crack, because it couldn't be seen enough to really be sure what it was. It could be just a piece of broken glass, but his wife was sure that it was her diamond wedding ring. Mr. Harper had to work carefully with his knife, because whatever it was it was stuck in there with some dirt that had wedged it tight. Finally, it began to move and loosen up and he extracted it from the crack and sure enough it was his wife's diamond wedding ring. She put it on her finger immediately without even cleaning the dirt from it and she hugged her husband and then gave him a big kiss and she began to cry with joy. Everyone else standing there was looking at the ring with their mouth open with surprise. The intoxicated man who had now sobered up exclaimed that he couldn't believe what he had just witnessed. Mr. Harper invited everyone to come into his house for coffee and they would discuss their experience with the Black woman and what the outcome of finding the wedding ring really meant. They all went into Mr. Harpers' house and his wife made coffee and then she started cleaning the ring in the sink with a toothbrush and some toothpaste. The now sober friend of Mr. Harper told them that the Black woman had not let him into her house and told him that he had been making fun of her all of the way to Victoria on their trip and that he needed to go and sit in the car, so that is what he did, but he was astonished as to how she had known that he had done that. They were all starting to see that the old Black woman was really someone that had some type of special power alright, but what was it they didn't know. She had told him what she shouldn't have known about, and she had directed them to the location of the diamond ring without actually being there herself. They all looked at Ben to tell about his experience with her and he told them all that she had said to him. Then he told them that on the way back to El Campo he had thought that she had been full of bull and that she was just a phony. He thought that she must have heard them talking on her front porch and picked up something that led her to tell the other man that he could not come in, but now since they had found the ring exactly like she had told Mr. Harper they would find it on top of what she had told Mr. Harper's friend Ben said that there was too much evidence that proved that she was authentic and that she had undoubtable told him the truth also about the Mexican cannon's that he had been looking for since his youth. Ben told them that what she told him should discourage him forever from looking for the cannon's ever again, but that it had the opposite effect on him. He told them that now that he knew the Fortune Teller was telling the truth it made him sure that the Mexican treasure in those cannon's really existed and that they were buried where the Mexican Cowboys had told in their stories by their campfires long ago, so now he knew that he would be looking for the real thing not just a made-up tale from the old days. Ben told them that he was going to continue to search for the fabulous Mexican treasure cannons.

CHAPTER FIVE-FINAL THOUGHTS

Blackie and Velma, my mother and father, had related this story to me otherwise I would never have believed it if I had heard it from someone else. I still believe it is true. They never told me if Ben found the Mexican treasure cannons, but I presume that he never did, or it would have been a very well-known event in El Campo and Wharton County's history.

Just think that fabulous Mexican treasure of gold and silver coins stuffed into two cannon is still waiting to be found and if they are then another piece of the puzzle of history will be solved.

The End

IT HAPPENED AGAIN: "IN EL CAMPO, TEXAS"
#2
Another True Story About a Supernatural Happening

CHAPTER ONE-HOW IT STARTED

It seems that there were strange things happening in El Campo, Texas back in the 1930's and 1940's. I have already told you the story about the Mexican cannons filled with gold and silver coins that were buried on the west bank of the Colorado River on the Blue Creek Ranch by the Mexican Army in 1836 and the quest to find them by Ben Peterson in the 1930's.

My father C.T. (Blackie) Blankenburg owned a small gasoline filling station during the Great Depression years in the 1930's. My mother Velma Blankenburg was teaching school at a country school and their combined income was one hundred dollars a month. With this they managed to buy some small calves for one dollar each and put them on a nurse cow to be grown out and sold with the money to be reinvested into cows that grew steadily until my father had enough cattle to be able to sell his filling station and go into full time cattle ranching in 1939. At this time, he was running some big steers along with his cows. The steers were to be sold at the Port City Stock Yard in Houston, Texas. My father would buy these steers when they were less than a year old and then graze them until they were two years old, and they weighed around 1,200 pounds. This had been a good addition for him with his cow-calf operation, because he could earn extra money with them between the roundup and sale of his calf crop.

CHAPTER TWO-THE REITZ POOL HALL

There was a popular Pool Hall in El Campo at the time in the 1940's owned by Antone Reitz. Antone Reitz at one time had been the Sheriff of Wharton County so he always carried a bone handled, blued Colt 45 revolver stuck in his belt at his waist partly hidden by a lite weight suit coat. He was a stern man and didn't put up with any guff from any-one. He had pool tables and domino tables there, but he sold no alcoholic beverages. He would let the men bring in their beer and whisky and he would sell them setups to mix with their whisky. Antone Reitz did not allow any women in his Pool Hall for any reason. It was totally the domain of men. My father liked to go there when he had time after he was through working on the ranch in the late afternoon. He liked to play dominoes and drink his whisky there with some of his friends. I remember this Pool Hall fondly, because it brings back thoughts of my father and also, I actually played pool there myself when I was in High School in the 1950's.

When I was a small boy and my father was at the Reitz Pool Hall playing dominos in the early 1940's late in the evenings my mother would gather me up and we would drive in the 1940 Chevrolet coupe to the Reitz Pool Hall to see when my father was going to come home for supper, so my mother would be able to have it hot and ready for him when he got home. This was stranded procedure for a lot of wives to do in those days. When we arrived at the Pool Hall, we would pull over to the curb and be in line with several other cars that wives and children were there to do the same thing with their husbands. You could compare this to being in line waiting to pull up to a drive through window today. As the cars in front of us would get to talk to their husbands they would drive off and the next car in line would pull up and would continue until it would be our turn to talk to Antone Reitz. He was in his 60's and was of average height with piercing blue eyes, a hook nose and a complexion that had a lot of brown spots from age and the weather. He would be sitting outside on a tall stool and as we pulled up, he would look at the car and know which man to call to inside the Pool Hall. He would lean forward and spit a stream of tobacco juice into a spittoon that was stationed at the side of his stool, and he would yell in the big, tall screen door "Blackie" and my father would come out and my mother would question him as to when she could expect him for supper then we would drive back home and get everything ready for our supper. I will never forget those times. Women now days would never consider doing anything like that, but in those days women and men had more of defined rolls in how they were organized into family life, and it was all understood and therefore it all worked very smoothly.

CHAPTER THREE-SCREW WORMS

Screw worms have been a terrible menace to all warm-blooded animals and also to humans through the centuries. They are flesh eating larva of a blow fly that live in warm climates. The blow fly lays its eggs on any spot of the animal that has blood on it from a wound or even the navel of a newborn animal, because the navel always has some blood around it right after birth. The eggs then hatch, and the larva start to bore into the flesh, and these are the screw worms. When these tiny new larvae start boring into the animal's flesh, they cause more blood to seep from the wound that attracts more blow flies to lay more eggs on that same place. As these larvae bore deeper onto the flesh, they grow in size then the new eggs hatch and a new hatch of tiny larvae began boring into the same area and this same process continues until the animal is treated and the screw worms are killed or the successive hatches of screwworms become numerous and bore so deep into the animals body that they finally kill the animal through excessive damage to the animal's body and organs or to infection caused by the weakening of the animal. This scourge to livestock also takes its toll on all wild animals. You can see that it was a major problem for all animals and humans that lived in warm climates. There was a season for screw worms in Texas that ran from when it warmed up in the spring until the first frost. There were no screw worms in the cold weather of winter, because the blow flies migrated back down south into Mexico, Central America and

South America. Dealing with the screw worms in livestock for ranchers was a constant problem that required being alert every day, during warm weather for screw worm infections and trying to catch and treat the animal as soon as possible to stop the damage the worms were causing. One of the main targets of the screw worm blow flies was that of a newborn calf laying their eggs around the navel cord, so the larva when they hatch could immediately bore into the soft flesh around the navel. This was a prime location that the worms would infect the newborn calves and they would cause the death of the calves within a matter of a couple of weeks. The longer the worms were left to do their damage before being treated the harder it was to kill all of them, because of the successive layers there were of them in the wound and also there was the chance of an infection on top of the damage to the flesh itself. Some of the calves were lucky if they had a mother cow that was more attentive to their young, because the mother cow would constantly lick the calf's navel area while it was still wet, bloody and soft before it dried and became tough to lick off the eggs that the blow fly had laid there. This would save the baby calf from being infected with the larva and the eggs were destroyed in the mother cow's digestive system. This was however not always the case because not all mother cows were that attentive to licking the navel area for several days while the navel dried up and fell off. During this screw worm season is when most of the new calves were born and the ranchers had to be on the lookout for newborn calves on a daily basis so they could be caught and doctored as soon as possible. That meant that the rancher, if he was a small operator, had to ride pasture himself, or if he was a larger rancher, he had to have someone riding his pastures every day to rope and catch the newborn calves and doctor them.

This is not as simple a job as it might seem. Someone unfamiliar with catching a newborn calf would think that the newborn calf being small and relatively weak in strength would be easy to subdue, but there are other considerations that have to be taken into account. The cowboy always carried with him in his saddle bags everything that he needed to doctor calves or grown animals for screw worms. That consisted of a bottle of chloroform to kill the worms, a big ball of cotton to put on the wound after applying the chloroform to smother the larva, a package of toothpicks to pick out the dead larva from the wound and a jar of 335 thick jelly to smear in and around the wound to keep the blow flies from relaying their eggs back on the wound. The cowboy would also have as part of his equipment his roping rope, his bat-wing leather chaps to protect him and his pistol on his hip in case, he had to defend himself and his horse from being gored by the mother cow and a pigging string, usually a small soft rope to tie the calf's legs if necessary.

CHAPTER FOUR-LOCATING THE NEWBORN CALF

When looking for a newborn calf there are several different scenarios that a cowboy learns to recognize. First is when he sees a cow standing well away from the herd by herself. The cow may be sick, crippled or she may have had a calf. Usually, a cow will go away from the herd to have a calf, so the calf doesn't get stepped on by other cows and also when the calf gets up to nurse of his mother's milk that he doesn't get confused and tries to nurse on another cow who would not allow it and would then knock the calf away with her horns and this would hurt the calf. When riding up to a lone cow the cowboy would be able to tell if she had recently had a new calf by observing the rear of the cow to see if he could see and blood and evidence of some afterbirth still hanging to the cow and also by observing the cow's milk bag to see of any of her tits had been nursed on. If one had been nursed by the calf it would look smaller and cleaner, then the other three tits. This was what he would like to see, because it would mean that the calf was healthy and strong, and the mother cow had her calf hidden and bedded down until it was time for the calf to nurse again. The problem now for the cowboy was to find the calf and doctor it for screw worms. To do this the cowboy had to learn calf language. The cowboy would ride a wide circle around the mother cow, and he would make the bellowing sound of a calf that was in distress. This would catch the attention of the mother cow and when the cowboy would get in the direction of her calf she would start walking fast in that direction. When that happened, the cowboy knew that he was near to her calf, and he would increase the volume of his voice to keep the cow interested. The cowboy had to keep a close eye on the cow, because if the calf was between the cow and the cowboy the cow might just drop her head for a few seconds to smell her calf to see if he was alright and she would keep walking to distract the cowboy from locating her calf. The cowboy would have to be able to keep his eye on the exact spot that the cow dropped her head so he could ride over to it and find her calf.

If the cowboy was lucky, he could dismount while the calf was sleeping and gently look the calf over to see if he had any screw worms without disturbing the calf enough to put it in distress and the cowboy could just put the 335 jelly on the navel of the calf and then mount his horse without even causing the mother cow to become aware that he had found her calf. On the other hand if the calf woke up and was afraid and got up and started bellowing and his mother cow started running to his aid then the cowboy would have to rope the calf and pull him onto the saddle with him and ride fast to get away from the mother cow and while she was searching around the place she had hidden her calf the cowboy would have time to doctor the calf and then take the calf back to the cow and drop him off close to her so they could reunite together before she would lead her calf off to another location. This situation could sometimes be extremely dangerous, because if the cowboy was not fast enough the cow could gore his horse or even himself. It was always touch and go in these situations. Large animals infected with screw worms would have to be roped put into trailers and hauled to the cattle pens to be doctored, or they would have to be roped by two cowboys on two different horses, this procedure was called heading and healing, because one cowboy would rope the horns on the animals head and the other would rope the two hind legs and then they would stretch the animal out using their horses to pull each rope tight and animal would fall over flat on the ground and then it could be held there and doctored. All of this required a lot of skill to try and avoid as much danger as possible to the cowboy and his horse.

The Brahma breed of cattle were better about dealing with screw worms and insects in general then the European breeds. They had the genetic ability to be able to shake their skin when flies and mosquitos bothered them to disrupt the insect's ability to bite them and the Brahman also had the ability to sweat, and it had a sort of insect repellant in the sweat. They would transfer this genetic ability to their offspring even if they had been bred to a European breed. The more Brahman blood the offspring had the more apt it would have to possess these insect fighting characteristics. Brahman cows were better mothers in general then the European breed of cows were. The Brahman cow was more apt to keep her newborn calf clean by licking it all over and that included licking the very vulnerable navel cord area that the blow flies liked to lay their eggs on. When licking the navel cord area, the mother cow would lick off any eggs that the blow fly had laid, and these eggs would be destroyed in the cow's digestive system. When the cow kept the navel area clean until the navel cord dried up and came off then the calf was safe from the blow flies. The cow's ability to keep her calf clean was the main deterrent to its safety from screw worms.

| 44 |

CHAPTER FIVE-WISHING AWAY THE SCREW WORMS

My father C.T. (Blacky) Blankenburg finally got the chance to take his pickup and horse to a pasture he had not had the chance to ride for two weeks, because it had been raining for several days and the black dirt road that took him there had turned into a mud quagmire. The road had finally firmed up enough so he would not get stuck going there on it. He unloaded his horse and opened the gate and went through closed the gate behind him mounted his horse that he had named Stardust, because she was a strawberry roan (red with white flecks). This was a rented pasture of 160 acres, and he had only big steers grazing in it. It had been an old homeplace that no one had lived there for many years, although the old broken-down house and sheds were still there. These steers were two years old, and a few were a few months older. He had thirty of them there and he expected to round them up and sell them in another six months. This day he was going to ride the fence and check to see that it was good then he was going to look over the steers to make sure none of them were sick and count them to make sure that they were all still in the pasture. As he was riding the fence, he noticed that the steers were in two bunches, and he could look over one bunch that was close to where he was riding on the west fence line. He counted twelve steers there and they all looked healthy, so he kept riding. He rounded the southern boundary and had to ride in a couple of hundred yards to look at the other bunch of steers. Here he only counted seventeen steers in this bunch, so he counted them again. They all looked healthy, but one steer was missing. He decided that he would finish riding the fence line before he went looking for the missing steer. After deciding that the fence was good, he rode over to where there was a low place that had some tall brush growing around it and sure enough the steer was there. He was momently relieved because he had found him until he jumped the steer up to see that the steer had evidently been tangled up in some old, barbed wire, because he was cut up on many places over his body and had a piece of barbed wire still wrapped around one hind leg and the steer had screw worms infected in all of these wounds. He even had screw worms in one of his ears, because he had that bloody drainage seeping out that screw worms produce when they are deep in the flesh. My father rode around the steer several times trying to assess the damage and trying to figure out what to do about it. He thought that this was a heck of a note, because this steer was to be sold soon and would have brought good money, but now he was just too infected in so many places that he could not be saved. He was very disappointed about this to say the least. By the time he rode back to his pickup and loaded his horse and took him back to where he belonged it was late in the afternoon, and he decided to go to Reitz Pool Hall, play some domino's, drink a little whisky and try to forget about that steer. He parked his pickup in the back of Reitz Pool Hall as usual reached behind the seat and retrieved his bottle of Old Crow whisky took off his spurs and entered the back door and went over to his usual table to wait for someone to come in that wanted to play dominos with him. The domino tables there had hollow legs with shelves in them that allowed the players to deposit their whisky bottles there to get them away from the top of the tables so they would not be in the way of the game. Antone Reitz knew all of his steady customers well and knew what they wanted for setups to mix their whisky with. He came over to the table where my father sat down and brought him his usual setup glass of ice and water. Blackie mixed his drink and seemed to drink it faster than usual waiting on some friends to join him. Garvin Park came in and joined him and then Marvin Bard came in and sat down. Now there were three of them and they could play three handed dominos. As the evening went on and Antone brought them new glasses of each one's favorite setup, he overheard the conversation between them that my father was telling Garvin and Marvin about the big steer he had found that was covered with infections of screw worms and that the steer was a hopeless case to try to cure. Antone stood there by my father for a few minutes and then told him that he might be able to help him with his screw worm problems. My father asked Antone what he meant by that and Antone told Blackie that if he would describe the steer to him, age, weight, color, any identifying marks such as spots of different colors or un-usual shapes of the horns then he could wish out the screw worms and that Blackie should not go and look at the steer for at least a week. Blackie thought that this was kind of strange, but he described the steer to Antone anyway then he told Antone that it would no good to look at the steer, because he would probably be dead in a week and all that he would see was a bunch of buzzards circling over the dead steer. Antone was insistent that Blackie should not look at the steer for at least a week and patted him on the shoulder in an expression of confidence in his abilities. Nothing more was said about it for the rest of the evening.

The next day my father resumed his normal activities dividing them between his small gasoline service station and his ranching. He had four pastures and would ride each one as his time would let him do it in an organized timetable so he could cover all of them in a reasonable number of days so he could stay on top of any trouble that might arise with the cattle such as sickness, being out of water, broken down fence, trouble with birthing a calf or screw worms. The days went by and it was time to go and look at the big steers again and he was dreading riding that pasture because he knew what he was going to see there. It was the middle of the afternoon by he got to the pasture and unloaded his horse. He saw that it looked like most of the steers were at the water troughs by the windmill, so he decided to ride there first to look at them. As he rode toward them, he was counting them, and he came up with the count of thirty, so he counted them again and it was thirty also. He thought that was impossible until he got a closer look, and he could not believe what his eyes were seeing. There was that steer right with the rest of them and all of his wounds were covered with scabs healing without any screw worms or infections. Blackie rode around the steer several times looking him over really good. He then remembered what Antone had told him about not going to look at the steer for at least a week, so he started to count the days from his evening at the Reitz Pool Hall and he came up with eight days. Blackie thought that this was crazy that it must be some sort of strange coincidence, but he knew how bad that steer had been, and it was impossible for him to be healed by himself. He rode the fence line as fast as he could, loaded his horse and took him back to his stall and drove to the Reitz Pool Hall as fast as he could get there. He needed to ask Antone some questions about this. My father was really confused, trying to understand what he had just seen with his own eyes and what Antone had told him eight days ago.

CHAPTER 6-THE SCREW WORM BUSINESS DEAL

Blackie drove his pickup behind the Reitz Pool Hall in his usual parking place reached behind the seat and retrieved his bottle of Old Crow whisky and sauntered in the back door with hopes that he could talk to Antone without being interrupted so he could get some answers to his questions about the miraculous healing of the big steer from the screw worms. As luck would have it Antone was sitting behind his counter and the Pool Hall was empty. Blackie sat down at the table that he liked, and Antone came over with the setup that he liked to mix his whiskey with. Blackie told Antone that he had seen the steer and that it had scabs covering all of the screw worm infected wounds and there was not any sign of any screw worms in the steer. He wanted to know what Antone could have done, if anything, to accomplish this or was it just some coincidence that happened at the same time as what Antone had told him about. Antone sat down with him and told him that he had the power to wish out the screw worms and he had given Blackie a free example of what he could do. Antone then told him that for two dollars per animal he would be able to wish out screw worms from any animal that Blackie would describe to him. Blackie sat there and listened to him and asked how he was able to do this, and Antone told him that he had received this special power from a lady that he had known for some time and that he was trying to get together some ranchers to use his services for a business. Antone told him that if he ever failed to cure an animal then he would refund the money, so there was not anything to lose. Blackie soon saw the benefit of this business deal and decided to use Antone from now on to cure the worst and hardest cases of screw worms. He would doctor the easiest ones himself and save that money. Blackie had a very enjoyable evening at the Pool Hall playing dominos and drinking his whisky.

Time went on and Blackie brought difficult cases of screw worms to Antone to heal, and Antone never failed him. This was saving him quite a lot of money and much needed time. This turned out to be a real blessing, because for two and one-half years Blackie was able to expand his herd of cattle and lease more pastures for grazing without having to spend all that extra time doctoring the bad screw worm cases and he didn't lose money with the bad cases dying, so it was a win, win all the way around until one evening he went to the Reitz Pool Hall to tell Antone about a cow that had a bad case of screw worms. He parked in the back of the Pool Hal as usual and retrieved his Old Crow whisky went in to get a domino table and talk to Antone. There were a few costumers inside the playing pool and a couple of domino tables occupied. He hailed greetings to the regular people he knew and sat down. Antone brought over his usual set up and Blackie motioned for him to sit down. He did and Blackie started to tell him about the cow with the screw worm infestation and Antone waved him off and told him that he could not help him anymore. Blackie frowned not really understanding what he was saying, and he tried to resume the description to Antone. He interrupted Blackie and asked him if he didn't understand what he told him. Blackie had a questioning expression on his face and Antone repeated that he would not be able to wish away screw worms anymore. Blackie was dumbfounded, because this business arrangement had worked so well and smoothly for so long that it seemed that it was impossible that it could end so abruptly.

Blackie ask Antone what had happened to bring all of this about and Antone just hung his head and told Blackie that it was all his own fault. He asked Antone what he had done, and Antone told him that he had tried to give the power to a friend of his and in the process, he had done it wrong. He told Blackie that his friend was a man and that he should not have tried to give it to a man because it was supposed to be passed from a man to a woman or from a woman to a man, but not from a man to a man or a woman to a woman. Blackie then asked him why he had tried to do it that way and Antone told him that he did not know that he would lose the power, but simply thought that if it didn't work that he just would not be able to pass it to his friend. As it happened though his friend did not receive the power and he lost the power in the process. Antone told Blackie that he was so sorry, but that nothing could be done about it. He had already consulted the woman that had transferred the power to him, and she told Antone that he would never be able to regain the power, because he had been so careless with it and that was that, just acccept it. Antone then got up to take care of some other customers and Blackie lifted his whisky bottle and took a long pull on it straight knowing that he was going to have to get back to doing the hard cases himself again and also probably losing money on some that would die.

CHAPTER 7-BLACKIES SCREW WORM PROBLEM ENDED

As a young cowboy my father, C.T. (Blackie) Blankenburg, had me riding pasture two to three days each week scouting for and doctoring cases of screw worms. He had a lung disease that prevented him from riding and doing hard manual labor, but he had taught me everything I needed to know about what to do. In the late 1950's there were experiments conducted irradiating male blow fly larva that proved to be beneficial in keeping the female fly from laying eggs that would hatch. The female flies would breed and only lay their eggs once in their lives and then they would die. Discovering this laid the groundwork for the final eradication of the screw worm scourge. A laboratory was finally built in Mission Texas in 1962 that was designed to irradiate thousands of these male screw worm fly larvae that would be sterile and then they would be released in areas that were experiencing screw worm infestations by small airplanes, thus breeding the female flies and leaving their eggs sterile so they would not hatch into screw worms. This proved to be so successful that the laboratory was expanded and eventually produced millions of sterile male flies to be released and by 1966 infestations were mostly under control. There were so many screw worm flies migrating in from Mexico, because they could fly 180 miles that it was realized something had to be done to stop that, so the program was expanded to release sterile male flies in Mexico and that helped, but then it was expanded further to include Guatemala and eventually was introduced into all of Central America. I always thought that this program was the only Government sponsored program that really worked, and it was relatively inexpensive and was administered very well. Since then, livestock producers and also wild game animals have been free of the screw worm scourge which has been worth untold wealth to livestock producers and to ranchers that make part of their living from leasing their range land for the hunting of wild game animals.

Blackie died in 1971, but he did live long enough to see the eradication of the screw worm and it wasn't from Supernatural powers, but from good science, although you might conclude that what inspired this was the wishes of all the livestock producers, so in the end it was a kind of wishing that cured the problem. Hmmmm wishing screw worms away, well maybe old Antone Reitz had something after all.

THE END

ABOUT THE AUTHOR

Paul A. Blankenburg was born in Dallas, Texas at Edna Gladney's Home for Unwed Mothers. He was adopted by a small rancher and his wife and raised in the Gulf Coast town of El Campo, Texas, graduated from El Campo High School, attended Wharton County Junior College, Graduated from Sam Houston State University in Huntsville, Texas with a BS Degree in Agriculture Science and Technology with a Minor in Biology and pursued a career in production ranching and farming, rural subdivision development, oil and gas leasing and finally retiring from the Texas Department Criminal Justice, moving out in the vast high mountains of the Chihuahua Desert where he resides today.

9 798218 141066